NORTHUMBRIA
a portrait in landscape

NORTHUMBRIA

a portrait in landscape

Photography by
Caroline and David Claughton

Introductions, captions
and poetry selection by
Gillian Dickinson

THE SPREDDEN PRESS

First published in 1994 by
The Spredden Press
Brocksbushes Farm
Stocksfield
Northumberland

ISBN Hardback   1 871739 30 6
ISBN Paperback   1 871739 29 2

Designed by Gill Humphrys, Durham
Printed and bound by Smith Settle, Ilkley Road, Otley,
West Yorkshire LS21 3JP

Contents

Acknowledgements

The publisher would like to thank the following for permission to reprint copyright material: Macmillan Publishers for 'Northumberland', 'Yeavering Bell' and 'Hareshaw' by Wilfrid Wilson Gibson; Oxford University Press for Poem No. 10 ('Stones trip Coquet Burn') and lines from **Briggflatts** from **Collected Poems** (1978) by Basil Bunting; Margaret Wilkes for lines from 'In the Cheviots' from **In an Old House** (Oriel Press, 1969); the estate of J. Phoenice for 'The Shining Strand' from **From the Kyloe Hills** (Oriel Press, 1970); J. C. Grant for lines from 'Alnwick' and 'The Tides of Tyne' from **Plough and Coble** (Oriel Press, 1967); and William Conton for lines from **The African** (Heinemann Educational Books, 1960).

We have been unable to trace the owners of copyright in the work of J. Phoenice, J. C. Grant and William Conton and would be grateful if they would contact the publisher.

The contents of the introduction and captions owe a great deal to the two volumes in Pevsner's Buildings of England series, mentioned at the end of the English introduction.

North Northumberland and the Coast

1. Berwick-upon-Tweed from the south
2. Old Bridge at Berwick-upon-Tweed
3. Royal Border Bridge at Berwick-upon-Tweed
4. Ford Church
5. Norham Castle
6. The Cheviot from Cold Law
7. Chillingham Castle
8. Lindisfarne Priory
9. Lindisfarne Castle
10. Bamburgh Castle
11. The beach at Bamburgh
12. The harbour at Seahouses
13. Beadnell harbour
14. The Cheviots and Wooler
15. Dunstanburgh from Embleton Bay
16. Roughting Linn

The Aln, Coquet and the Wansbeck

17. Alnwick Castle from the river Aln
18. Hulne Priory
19. Alnwick Castle from the Lion Bridge
20. Edlingham Castle
21. Cup-and-ring rock on Garleigh Moor
22. Warkworth Castle
23. Amble Harbour
24. The Coquet river, near Shillmoor
25. Cragside
26. Brinkburn Priory
27. The Cheviots from Simonside Hill
28. Harbottle Castle
29. Lady's Well, Holystone
30. Morpeth Court House
31. Bothal Castle
32. Mitford Castle
33. Newminster Abbey
34. Belsay Quarry Garden
35. Belsay Castle
36. Wallington Hall
37. Bolam Lake
38. Elsdon

The Tyne and Hadrian's Wall

39. Hadrian's Wall west of Housesteads
40. The Wall at Winshields Crag
41. The Wall at Walltown Crags
42. Black Middens bastle, Tarset Burn
43. Kielder Water
44. Blanchland Abbey
45. Hexham Abbey
46. Chesters Bath House
47. Chollerford
48. Corbridge from river
49. Corbridge from Roman town
50. Aydon Castle
51. Dilston Castle
52. Matfen standing stone
53. Chipchase Castle
54. Prudhoe Castle
55. St Andrew's church, Bywell
56. Langley Castle
57. Allen Banks
58. Hareshaw Linn, near Bellingham

Tyneside, Teesdale and the Wear

59. Durham Cathedral from South Street
60. The Gatehouse, Durham Castle
61. Durham Cathedral from river Wear
62. Bishop Auckland Palace
63. The Deer House, Bishop Auckland Palace
64. Escomb Church
65. Finchale Priory
66. Killhope Lead Mining Centre
67. Weardale
68. Barnard Castle
69. Bowes Museum
70. Egglestone Abbey
71. High Force Waterfall
72. Washington Old Hall
73. Raby Castle
74. Seaton Delaval Hall
75. Marsden Rock
76. Tynemouth Priory
77. The Black Gate, Newcastle upon Tyne
78. The Civic Centre, Newcastle upon Tyne
79. Tyneside Maritime Festival
80. Tall Ships at Quayside. Newcastle upon Tyne

Introduction

This is a collection of 80 photographs of the countryside and historic buildings of Northumbria, a tourist area which now includes the counties of Northumberland, Tyne and Wear and Durham.

Caroline and David Claughton are two young photographers now living in Wetherby, Yorkshire. They have been photographing in Northumbria for several years, but because the region is so rich in scenery, and in the diversity of its buildings and monuments, the selection of photographs has not been easy. The English Border country is a land of stone walls, moors, hills and long sandy beaches; a land much fought over, and defended by an impressive number of castles, bastles* and fortified manor houses, many of them built of stone taken from the most dramatic monument of all, Hadrian's Wall.

This short introduction to Northumbria aims to help you to choose itineraries to the most interesting sites. The book is divided into geographical sections, each introduced by a few poems inspired by events or by the countryside.

The Roads from the North

There are three main routes into England from Scotland. Two, the A68 and the A1, follow Roman roads for much of the way. They come together in the south-east of the county to join the motorways south. The furthest west, and the most dramatic road, is the A68 which crosses the Border high in the Cheviots at Carter Bar and enters the Northumberland National Park. It joins the Roman Dere Street near Rochester and follows it, arrow-straight, through Redesdale, switch-backing over ridges of land to cross the Wall, and the Military Road, north of Corbridge.

The second is the 18th-century turnpike road, the A697, which crosses the Tweed at Coldstream, between two of the great Border castles, Norham to the north and Wark-on-Tweed to the south. East of the road and the river Till are the 14th-century castles of Ford, Etal and Chillingham. To the west is Flodden where, in 1513, the greatest battle in Northumbrian history was fought and King James IV and the elite of Scotland were killed. A few miles south of Flodden is Yeavering where, in the 7th century, King Edwin of Northumbria had his wooden palace.

The third route south is probably best known: the Great North Road, now the A1, which, like the main east-coast railway, passes through the town of Berwick-upon-Tweed. The road continues to Alnwick, Morpeth and the motorway south while the railway hugs the coast, giving the train passenger many spectacular views. Described as both the most romantic and most exciting of Northumbrian towns, Berwick changed hands many times and perhaps for that reason was mentioned separately in Acts of Parliament up to 1746 though it has been English since 1482. Its grand and immensely strong Elizabethan fortifications still bear witness to its turbulent past.

The Coast

From the A1 you can discover the many attractions of the coast. Holy Island (Lindisfarne) is reached by a causeway across the sands and is only accessible at low tide. Here St Aidan came from Iona in 634 AD to establish a monastery and convert the kingdom of Northumbria to Celtic Christianity. His successor was St Cuthbert and it was in his memory that the monks created the Lindisfarne Gospels (now in the British Museum), with their wonderful decorated pages. The first monastery of St Aidan and St Cuthbert was destroyed by Danes but ruins of the great red sandstone priory church, built at the same time as Durham Cathedral, still stand. Lindisfarne Castle, restored by the architect Edwin Lutyens at the beginning of this century, is open to visitors.

St Cuthbert lived for some years as a hermit on the remote Inner Farne, the largest of the Farne Islands, where he died in 687 AD. The Farne Islands are a national bird sanctuary, renowned for their colonies of sea-birds and grey seals. They can be reached by boat from Seahouses.

The Northern Castles

Between Berwick and Newcastle three great castles defend the coast: Bamburgh, Dunstanburgh and Warkworth. Bamburgh is poised high above the sea on an outcrop of the volcanic rock known as the Whin Sill. It has provided a perfect site for defence since the Iron Age. Dunstanburgh, whose gatehouse was built after the

English lost Berwick to the Scots at Bannockburn in 1314, is now a dramatic ruin, defended from the north by steep cliffs. Warkworth, near the mouth of the Coquet, has belonged to the Percys of Alnwick since 1332 (Percy is the family name of the Dukes of Northumberland).

The Coquet and the Wansbeck

Alnwick, ducal town of Northumberland and seat of the Percys since 1309, is entered from the north by the 18th-century Lion Bridge over the Aln, with its view across the park created by the Northumbrian-born landscape designer, Lancelot (Capability) Brown. The southern entrance is through the Hotspur gate, part of the old town walls. The castle, which dates from the 12th century or earlier, has been added to and altered up to the 19th century and has a rich collection of 18th-century paintings. Hulne Park, which belongs to the Duke, has the remains of a 13th-century Carmelite priory protected by a 15th-century curtain wall. It is well worth visiting — but note that only pedestrians are allowed in the park and there is a lot of walking.

Alnwick is probably the best centre for exploring the coast. The nearest coastal town is Alnmouth, a planned medieval port until 1806 when the Aln changed course and the harbour silted up. A few miles further south, the Coquet, 'loveliest of wandering, winding Northumbrian streams', enters the sea at Amble. From Alnwick, a beautiful road across the moors takes you to the attractive small town of Rothbury, made fashionable at the end of the 19th-century by nearby Cragside. This was the dramatic seat of the first Lord Armstrong and the first house in the world to be lit by hydro-electric power. It is one of the most frequently visited of National Trust properties.

A few miles east of Rothbury, almost surrounded by a loop of the river, is the 12th-century priory of Brinkburn, convincingly restored in the 19th century. Here, in 1991, a re-enactment of the first performance of Monteverdi's Vespers was recorded for television.

If you are in this part of Coquetdale it is worth continuing west into Northumberland National Park to Elsdon, the capital of Redesdale in the Middle Ages. It is still a remote area of many sheep and few farms. With the completion of the New Line, the direct road from Belsay to Otterburn (now part of the A696) in 1836, Elsdon was bypassed and lost its importance. Unusually for Northumberland, it has a village green, which is dominated by the church and a fortified 14th-century tower. Nearby is a huge earthwork, probably built — like that at Harbottle — by the Umfraville family in the 12th century.

To reach Holystone and Harbottle, two attractive villages in some of the most peaceful and beautiful country in Northumberland, you leave the Rothbury-Elsdon road at Swindon and follow the Coquet river upstream. A short walk from Holystone village is the Lady's Well, once used by travellers on the road across Redesdale to the coast and sacred to the border saint, Ninian.

The centre of Morpeth, the county town, is surrounded on three sides by the Wansbeck and has suffered several times when the river has flooded. In the Market Place there is a fine Town Hall by Vanburgh and to the south of the town are the remains of two castles. Don't miss the unique Bagpipe Museum in the town. Nearby are the romantic ruins of Newminster Abbey, an important Cistercian monastery, and Mitford Castle — both date from the 12th century.

Two of the most interesting country houses open to the public can be easily reached from Morpeth. Belsay, home of the Middletons for six centuries, with its 14th-century castle, its Grecian Hall begun in 1807 and its unusual and beautiful gardens, has been described as an 'encapsulation of English history'. Wallington, which has belonged to three notable Northumbrian families, the Fenwicks, the Blacketts and the Trevelyans, is now largely an 18th-century house with 19th-century alterations by the Trevelyan family. The gardens, across the road, were designed, c. 1760, by Capability Brown who went to school in the estate village, Cambo.

Much of the country between Morpeth and Newcastle was coal country, and Blyth, at the mouth of the river of that name, was an important coal port. It also had two shipyards. To the south is Seaton Delaval, gaunt and smoke-blackened by two severe fires, yet the most powerful of Vanburgh's houses. Tynemouth, whose castle and priory date from the 11th century, remained a fortress long after the dissolution of its monastery. Its sandstone ruins, pitted by sea-spray and now cared for by English Heritage, stand above precipitous cliffs.

Newcastle

Newcastle is the city of the Tyne as London is of the Thames. It has been an important city since the Romans built the first bridge over the river in the late 2nd century. In the 19th century its great shipbuilding works and its supremacy in the coal trade provided much of the lifeblood of the nation. It was at this time that the distinctive city centre you can see today was created by Richard Grainger and John Dobson. Ships have always been important to the Tyne and it is fitting that Newcastle, once the home of great sailing ships, should regularly act as host to the Tall Ships race.

The Tyne

The Tyne is the main artery of Northumberland, and throughout recorded history most of the county's population has settled along the banks of the river. The ancient and beautiful market town of Hexham, situated close to the confluence of the North and South Tyne, has been described as 'the heart of all England'. Certainly it is the centre of Tynedale and an ideal place from which to explore Roman remains, castles, Saxon churches and country houses. Hexham's priory church, known as the Abbey, dates from the 12th century, and replaced the earlier church, founded by Wilfrid, which was sacked by the Danes. There is much to explore in this historic town.

To the east is Corbridge, with its Roman garrison town and Saxon church. An important medieval market place, today the village again attracts discerning shoppers from miles around. Between Corbridge and Hexham, on a small tributary of the Tyne, are the remains of Dilston castle, home of the last Earl of Derwentwater who was executed in 1716 for his part in the Jacobite rebellion. A mile to the north, on the steep banks of the Cor Burn, is Aydon Castle and, on the line of the Wall and built from its stones, Halton tower.

Corbridge has the only bridge over the Tyne to have withstood the flood of 1771. The next old bridge to the east is at Bywell, a lovely, peaceful spot with a castle and two churches dating from Saxon times. Only a market cross survives to remind one of the village whose population was moved to Stocksfield when Bywell Hall was built.

Ovingham, with another Saxon tower, is close to Cherryburn, birthplace of the artist and naturalist, Thomas Bewick. Bewick is buried in Ovingham churchyard. Wylam, a village straddling the Tyne, is the home of the great railway engineer, George Stephenson, whose house can be visited (like Cherryburn, it is the property of the National Trust). To the south the important 14th-century castle of Prudhoe dominates the river, close to the town which was a mining community for five centuries.

North of the Tyne valley, Hadrian's Wall crosses the country from Wallsend near Newcastle to Bowness on the Solway. The Roman fort at Corbridge, built originally to guard the bridge carrying Dere Street across the Tyne, developed into a garrison town for soldiers on the Wall. The fort at Chesters (Cilurnum) was built to guard the Wall where it crosses the North Tyne: the remains of the Roman bridge can still be seen. The most spectacular part of the Wall, the section west of Sewingshields to Greenhead, which includes the celebrated fort of Housesteads, is built along the natural cliffs of the Whin Sill. West and south of Housesteads, on the Stanegate Road (the first Roman frontier in Britain) is Vindolanda, another fort and civilian settlement.

Returning along the Military Road (B6318) to Chollerford you can follow the North Tyne upstream to some of the best and most beautiful walking country in the county. Wark is the old capital of North Tynedale. Bellingham, home of the famous Bellingham Show, is certainly its centre now. 'Nowhere is the northern Tyne more beautiful than as it flows past this stone-built village, to receive, a little further on, the beautiful tributary, the Reed at Reedsmouth' *(Highways and Byways in Northumbria)*. To the west is Kielder with the largest forest and the largest man-made reservoir in Western Europe: this huge expanse of water blends better with the landscape than anyone could have hoped when the project was begun.

South of Hexham, you come quickly to open moorland, crossed by rivers. Blanchland, which lies in the wooded upper Derwent valley, is a charming village developed from monastic buildings in the 18th century by the Crewe trustees. The road continues past the southern shores of Derwent reservoir — the second largest in the country — and turns south to Stanhope in the Wear valley and Middleton-in-Teesdale.

Another road (the A686) leads past the National Trust

property of Allen Banks and Ridley woods where, if the weather is fine, you can have an enchanted walk. The road divides, south of Langley castle, to follow the two branches of the river Allen upstream, the west to Alston, the east to Allendale town and Allenheads, a tourist centre for exploring the Pennine moors. This is old lead-mining country and there are remains of many old workings. An exhibition at Killhope Lead Mining Centre recalls the history of this industry in fascinating detail.

Durham

As Newcastle is the city of the Tyne, Durham owes its historical preeminence to the river Wear which almost encircles the city. The bishops of Durham were princes of the church, lords of the County Palatine of Durham, with their own coinage, parliament, secular courts and armies throughout the Middle Ages, and the right to sit on the right hand of the king at his coronation. Their position was more like that of the Prince-Bishops of Germany than that of an English bishop. Their territory extended from Norham on the Scottish Border to Holy Island in the east.

Their private residence, since the 12th century, is the palace at Bishop Auckland, restored in the 18th century, after the devastation of the Civil War. The park is open to the public every day and the palace on selected days. North of Durham, beautifully situated in another loop of this meandering river, are the ruins of Finchale Priory.

About two miles (3.2 km) or so north of the A66, in the Tees valley, is the attractive town of Barnard Castle on whose outskirts is the extraordinary, French-inspired Bowes Museum, with its outstanding collection of Spanish paintings. High above the river Tees are the romantic remains of Egglestone Abbey. If you follow the Tees upstream, you come to the spectacular waterfalls at High Force in wonderful walking country.

The A688 will take you north-east from Barnard Castle to Raby, seat of the Nevilles, one of the great northern families whose lands were forfeited in 1569 because of the earl's part in the Northern Rising of that year. You can return to Durham, via Bishop Auckland, visiting on the way Escomb, one of the very rare complete Saxon churches to survive, and Witton Castle and Park. Between Durham and Newcastle, an oasis in the new town of Washington, is Washington Old Hall, the home of George Washington's ancestors and lovingly restored in 1937 with Anglo-American money.

Gillian Dickinson

*a small defensible house

Short Reading List

N. Pevsner, John Grundy, Grace McCombie, Peter Ryder, Humphrey Welfare and Stafford Linsley: **Northumberland** (2nd edn, 1992)

N. Pevsner, rev. E. Williamson: **County Durham** (2nd edn, 1983) Buildings of England series.

Ordnance Survey Leisure Guide to Northumbria (1987)

Peter Anderson Graham: **Highways and Byways in Northumbria** (1920; reprinted 1988)

David Archer: **Land of Singing Waters: Rivers and Great Floods of Northumbria** (1992)

David Breeze and Brian Dobson: **Hadrian's Wall** (3rd edn, 1987)

Stephen Johnson: **Hadrian's Wall** (1989)

C. M. Fraser and K. Emsley: **Northumbria** (2nd edn, 1989)

T. H. Rowland: **Medieval Castles, Towers, Peles and Bastles of Northumberland** (1987)

Northumberland National Park publishes a range of walks, guides and free information leaflets.

Introduction

La Northumbrie était l'ancien royaume de ces Britanniques qui vivaient au nord du fleuve du Humber, mais de nos jours c'est le nom donné à la région touristique comprenant à la fois les départements de Northumberland et de Durham.

Les 80 photographies dans ce livre, réalisées par les jeunes photographes, Caroline et David Claughton, ont pour but de vous introduire à la variété et à la beauté de cette région du Border. C'est un pays de murs en pierre, de landes et de longues plages de sable; un pays où l'on s'est beaucoup battu et qui a été défendu par un nombre impressionnant de châteaux, de 'bastles' *et de manoirs fortifiés, dont plusieurs construits de pierres appartenant au monument le plus spectaculaire de tous: la Muraille d'Hadrien.

Les rivières de la Tweed, de l'Aln, de la Wansbeck, du Coquet, de la Tyne et de la Tees, qui coulent toutes de l'ouest à l'est, divisent la contrée en régions traversées par trois routes principales (la A1, la A68 et la A697). Le voyageur peut ainsi parcourir cette région à partir du sud-est, plus peuplé, jusqu'à la frontière écossaise. Au sud de la région nous trouvons trois routes d'est à ouest qui donnent accès à tous les villages et sites principaux. Nous avons: la 'Military Road' (B6318) qui suit la Muraille d'Hadrien de Newcastle à Carlisle, la A69 qui borde la vallée de la Tyne du sud et, finalement, la A66 qui s'étend de l'ouest de Scotch Corner à Brough et Penrith.

La A1, connue pendant des siècles comme 'the Great North Road', à cause de son important traffic de carrosses, franchit le Border à Berwick-on-Tweed. Ses robustes fortifications temoignent d'un passé turbulent. Entre Berwick et Newcastle, trois grands châteaux gardent la côte: ceux de Bamburgh, Dunstanburgh et Warkworth.

Au nord de Bamburgh se trouve Holy Island (Lindisfarne), accessible à marée basse par une route au milieu du sable. C'est l'île de St Aidan et de St Cuthbert. St Aidan apporta la foi chrétienne de l'Iona au royaume de la Northumbrie en 634 après J.C. et la sainteté de St Cuthbert, son successeur, a été commemorée par la construction de la cathédrale de Durham.

La A1 continue vers le sud jusqu'à Alnwick, demeure des Percy, (nom de la famille du Duc de Northumberland) depuis six siècles. Alnwick est un bon point de départ pour explorer la côte. Une route à travers les landes vous amène à la petite ville de Rothbury, qui se trouve près de Cragside, demeure spectaculaire du premier Lord Armstrong et dont la maison fut la première au monde à être illuminée par énergie hydro-électrique. C'est une des propriétés du National Trust les plus frequemment visitées. Morpeth, chef-lieu séduisant sur la rivière de la Wansbeck, est à proximité de deux châteaux superbes: Belsay et Wallington, tous les deux ouverts au public.

A partir de Belsay, sur la A696, on peut continuer jusqu'à Otterburn, lieu d'une bataille commémorée par une ballade célèbre. La A696 rejoint ensuite la A68 qui traverse le Parc National et franchit le Border dans les Cheviots à Carter Bar. Une route secondaire vous amène d'Otterburn à Elsdon, avec sa demeure fortifiée datant du 14ème siècle et son joli parc, ainsi qu'à Holystone et Harbottle, endroits ravissants et rarement visités, se trouvant dans la vallée de la rivière du Coquet.

La A697 traverse la Tweed à Coldstream, entre deux grands châteaux du Border, Norham au nord et Wark-on-Tweed au sud. A l'est de cette route et de la rivière de la Till se trouvent les châteaux datants du 14ème siècle d'Etal, de Ford et de Chillingham. A l'ouest on rencontre Flodden, village qui à été témoin en 1513 d'une des plus grandes batailles de l'histoire du Northumberland et où le roi James IV et l'élite écossaise ont trouvé la mort.

Newcastle, que l'on rejoint à quelques minutes de Morpeth par la route, a été une ville importante depuis la fin du deuxième siècle, lorsque les Romains construirent le premier pont sur la Tyne. La ville possède de nos jours six ponts. Au 19ème siècle, l'importance de la construction navale et la suprématie du commerce de charbon on fait de Newcastle une ville primordiale, moteur de la nation entière. A cette époque Richard Grainger et John Dobson créèrent le centre de la ville, centre caractéristique qui mérite à être exploré.

La Tyne est l'artère principale du Northumberland; au cours de l'histoire la majorité de la population s'est établie le long de son rivage. L'ancienne et belle ville de Hexham, ville où se tient un marché, est située près du confluent de la Tyne du nord et de la Tyne du sud. Elle a été décrite comme ' le coeur de toute l'Angleterre'. Elle représente certainement le centre du Tynedale et un endroit idéal pour explorer les ruines romaines à Corbridge, les châteaux à Dilston, Aydon et Prudhoe et les églises saxonnes à Bywell, Corbridge et Ovingham. Vous pouvez aussi suivre la Tyne du Nord, à travers une belle campagne, jusqu'à Wark, Bellingham et arriver finalement à Kielder, un important centre touristique, où vous decouvrirez la plus grande forêt, ainsi que le plus grand réservoir, fabriqúe par l'homme, d'Europe Occidentale.

Au sud de Hexham, vous arriverez rapidement à un paysage de landes, découpées par des rivières. Le village de Blanchland, dans la vallée boisée du Derwent, s'est developpé à partir d'une fondation monastique. Vous entrez dans le village par une porte monumentale en pierre où réside aujourd'hui le bureau de poste. Il y a un excellent hotel: The Lord Crewe Arms.

Les deux affluents de la rivière Allen, provenant de la Tyne du Sud, offrent de jolies promenades dans la propriété du National Trust à Allen Banks et aux alentours d'Allenheads. Allenheads est le centre touristique pour explorer les 'North Pennine Moors'.

A quelques kilomètres au sud, vous arriverez à la vallée du Wear, connue autrefois principalement pour ses mines de plomb et ses carrières de calcaire. La ville de Durham, centre historique mondial, doit son importance historique au fleuve qui l'encercle presque entièrement. Durant le Moyen-Age, les évèques de Durham étaient Princes de l'Eglise, Seigneurs du Comté indépendant de Durham, avec leur propre monnaie, leur parlement, leur tribunal séculier et leurs armées. Leur territoire s'étendait de Norham sur la frontière écossaise à Holy Island à l'est. Depuis le 12ème siècle le palais de Bishop Auckland, construit sur la rivière, est leur demeure privée. Le palais est ouvert au public (mais pas tous les jours). Au nord de Durham, situées admirablement dans une autre boucle de ce fleuve sinueux, vous rencontrerez les ruines du Prieuré de Finchale.

Le joli village de Barnard Castle est à quelques kms de la A66 et dans ses environs vous trouverez un musée extraordinaire et d'inspiration française: le musée Bowes. Tout près, sur la rivière de la Tees, vous avez les ruines romantiques de l'Abbaye d'Egglestone. Si vous remontez cette rivière à l'amont, après une belle promenade, vous arriverez aux chutes spectaculaires de High Force.

La A688 vous amène au nord-est de Barnard Castle à Raby, demeure des Neville, une des grandes familles du Nord de l'Angleterre, dont les terres ont été confisquées à cause du rôle joúe par le Comté dans l'insurrection, 'the Northern Rising', de 1569. Vous pouvez revenir sur Durham, en passant par Bishop Auckland et visiter en cours de route Escomb, une des plus rares églises saxonnes de nos jours, ainsi que Witton Castle. Entre Durham et Newcastle vous recontrerez dans la ville moderne de Washington, une oasis: le 'Washington Old Hall', demeure des ancêtres de George Washington, qui a été restaurée avec beaucoup de soins en 1937, à l'aide de fonds anglo-americains.

* nom pour une petite maison fortifiée

Traduit par Simonetta Emiliani

Einleitung

Northumbrien war das alte Königreich der Briten, die nördlich des Flusses Humber lebten, aber heute ist es der Name einer Gegend, die viel von Touristen besucht wird und geographisch aus den Grafschaften Northumberland und Durham besteht.

Die 80 Fotografien in diesem Buch, die von den hervorragenden Fotografen Caroline und David Claughton aufgenommen wurden, haben das Ziel, Sie in die Schönheit und Vielfältigkeit des Landes, das an der englisch-schottischen Grenze liegt, einzuführen. Es ist ein Land der Steinmauern, bergiger Heidelandschaft und langer, sandiger Strände, ein Land um das stark gekämpft wurde und das von einer beeindruckenden Anzahl von Burgen, befestigten Häusern und Herrenhäusern verteidigt wurde, mehrere von diesen wurden aus Steinen gebaut, die von dem dramatischsten Monument aller, dem Hadrian's Wall, entfernt wurden.

Die Flüsse Tweed, Aln, Wansbeck, Coquet, Tyne and Tees fließen alle von Westen nach Osten und teilen das Land in Regionen, die von drei Haupstraßen (der A1, A68 und der A697) durchkreuzt werden, die den Besucher von dem stärker bevölkerten Südosten an die schottische Grenze bringen. Im Süden des Landes gibt es drei Straßen, die von Osten nach die Westen führen und über die hauptsächlichen Städte und Sehenswürdigkeiten leicht zu erreichen sind. Das sind die Militärstraße (Military Road, B6318), die dem Hadrians Wall von Newcastle nach Carlisle folgt, die A69, die durch das Tal der Südtyne führt und die A66, die von Scotch Corner nach Brough und Penrith in westlicher Richtung verläuft.

Die A1, die seit Jahrhunderten als Great North Road wegen ihrer Bedeutung als Poststraße bekannt ist, führt in Berwick-on-Tweed über die schottische Grenze. Die sehr starken Befestigungen dieser Stadt sind heute noch Zeugen einer turbulenten Vergangenheit. Drei großartige Burgen Bamburgh, Dunstanburgh und Warkworth beschützen die Küste zwischen Berwick and Newcastle.

Nördlich von Bamburgh liegt die Heilige Insel (Holy Island), die nur bei Ebbe über einen Damm, der über Sand führt, erreicht werden kann. Das ist die Insel des heiligen Aidans, der im Jahre 634 AD das Christentum von Iona nach Northumbrien brachte und auch die Insel von seinem Nachfolger, dem heiligen Cuthbert, in dessem Gedenken die Kathedrale in Durham gebaut wurde.

Die A1 führt in südlicher Richtung weiter nach Alnwick, seit sechs Jahrhunderten der Sitz der Herzöge von Northumberland, deren Familienname Percy ist. Alnwick ist sehr zentral gelegen und geeignet, um von dort aus die Küste zu entdecken. Eine Straße führt durch bergige Heidelandschaft nach der kleinen Stadt Rothbury, es ist ungefähr anderthalb Kilometer von Cragside entfernt, dem dramatischen Sitz des ersten Lord Armstrong und es ist das erste Haus in der Welt, das durch Wasserkraft erzeugte Energie beleuchtet wurde. Das ist eine der meist besuchten Stätten die dem National Trust gehören. Morpeth ist die attraktive Hauptstadt der Grafschaft, am Fluß Wansbeck gelegen. Morpeth liegt in der Nähe von zwei wunderschönen Landsitzen, Belsay und Wallington, die der Öffentlichkeit zugänglich sind.

Von Belsay können Sie in nördlicher Richtung auf der A696 nach Otterburn weiterfahren, der Stätte einer Schlacht, der in einer berühmten Ballade gedacht wird. Von da aus können Sie auf die landschaftlich schöne A68 stoßen, die die schottische Grenze hoch in den Cheviot Bergen am Carter Bar überquert . Von Otterburn führt eine kleine Nebenstraße durch das Dorf Elsdon mit einem Haus und seinem Turm, das aus dem 14. Jahrhundert stammt, sowie einem Dorfanger. Diese Straße führt weiter nach Holystone und Harbottle, das in dem lieblichen und selten besuchten oberen Abschnitt des Coquettales liegt.

Die A697 überquert den Fluß Tweed in Coldstream, das zwischen zwei großartigen Grenzburgen, Norham im Norden und Wark-on-Tweed im Süden, liegt. Östlich dieser Straße und des Flusses Till liegen die Burgen Etal, Ford und Chillingham. Im Westen liegt Flodden, wo im Jahre 1513 die größte Schlacht in der Geschichte Northumberlands ausgetragen wurde, bei der König James der Vierte und die Elite Schottlands ums Leben kamen.

Von Morpeth braucht man heute nur ein paar Minuten auf der Schnellstraße, um nach Newcastle zu kommen. Newcastle ist seit der Zeit wichtig, in der die Römer am Ende des 2. Jahrhunderts die erste Brücke über die Tyne bauten. Die Stadt hat jetzt sechs Brücken. Im 19. Jahrhundert waren die großen Werften und Newcastle's Vorherrschaft im Kohlehandel äußerst wichtig für die ganze Nation. Zu dieser Zeit schafften Richard Grainger und John Dobson das bemerkenswerte Stadtzentrum, es lohnt sich, es zu entdecken.

Die Tyne ist die Hauptarterie von Northumberland und soweit man in der Geschichte zurückdenken kann, hat sich die Bevölkerung an den Ufern des Flusses angesiedelt. Die alte und schöne Marktstadt Hexham liegt in der Nähe des Zusammenflusses der Süd- und Nordtyne. Hexham is als „das Herz von ganz England" beschrieben worden. Es ist auf jeden Fall das Zentrum des Tynedales und ein idealer Ort von dem aus man die römischen Ausgrabungen in Corbridge, die Burgen in Dilston, Aydon und Prudhoe sowie die altsächsischen Kirchen in Bywell, Corbridge und Ovingham erforschen kann. Sie könnten auch der Nordtyne durch schöne Landschaft nach Wark, Bellingham und schließlich nach Kielder folgen, wo Sie den größten Forst und die größte künstlich angelegte Talsperre, die es in Westeuropa gibt, entdecken — es ist ein großer Anziehungspunkt für Touristen.

Südlich von Hexham kommen Sie schnell zu offener Heidelandschaft, die von Flüssen durchquert wird. Das Dorf Blanchland in dem bewaldeten Derwenttal entwickelte sich durch eine Klosterstiftung und man kommt durch einen großen Torweg, der aus Stein gebaut ist, der jetzt das Postamt beherbergt. Es gibt dort ein ausgezeichnetes Hotel, das Lord Crewe Arms heißt. Die zwei Arme des Flusses Allen, der ein Nebenfluß der Südtyne ist, laden zu wunderschönen Spaziergängen durch den Besitz des National Trusts in Allen Banks und in der Umgebung von Allenheads ein. Allenheads ist auch ein Touristenzentrum für die Erforschung der Heidelandschaft der Penninen.

Sie erreichen das Weartal, wenn Sie ein paar Kilometer nach Süden fahren. Früher war das Weartal für seine Bleibergwerke und Kalksteinbrüche bekannt. Die Stadt Durham ist eine Stadt, die zu dem Erbgut der Welt (World Heritage Centre) gehört. Durham verdankt seine vorrangige Stellung dem Fluß, der die Stadt fast einkreist. Durch das Mittelalter hindurch waren die Bischöfe von Durham Prinzen der Kirche, Herren über die selbständige Pfalzgrafschaft Durham, man kann das

mit den Bischöfen der Pfalzgrafschaften in Deutschland vergleichen, diese Machtstellung der prinzlichen Bischöfe gab es in keinem anderen Land Europas. Die Pfalzgrafschaft Durham hatte sein eigenes Münzrecht, Parlament, eigene Gerichtsbarkeit und Armeen. Ihr Gebiet erstreckte sich von Norham an der schottischen Grenze bis Holy Island im Osten.

Seit dem 12. Jahrhundert ist der private Wohnsitz der Bischöfe der Palast in Bishop Auckland, der hoch über Fluß gebaut ist. Er ist der Öffentlichkeit zugängig (aber nicht jeden Tag). Nördlich von Durham ist die wunderschöne, an einer anderen Schleife des sich dahinwindenden Flusses, gelegene Ruine der Klosterkirche Finchale.

Ungefähr 5 km nördlich der A66 ist die anziehende kleine Stadt Barnard Castle. Am Stadtrand ist das außergewöhnliche, nach französichem Stil gebaute Bowes Museum. Es hat eine hervorragende Sammlung spanischer Gemälde. Ganz in der Nähe finden Sie die romantischen Überreste der Egglestone Abtei. Wenn Sie dem Fluß stromauf folgen, kommen sie zum hochdramatischen Wasserfall in High Force, er liegt in einem wunderschönen Wandergebiet.

Die A688 wird Sie in nord-östlicher Richtung von Barnard Castle nach Raby bringen, Sitz der Nevilles, eine der bedeutenden Familien des Nordens, deren Ländereien als Buße konfiziert wurden, wegen der Rolle, die der Graf im Jahre 1569 bei einem Aufstand im Norden gespielt hatte. Sir können über Bishop Auckland nach Durham zurückkehren und auf dem Wege Escomb, eine der sehr seltenen altsächsischen Kirchen, die noch überleben und Burg Witton besuchen. Washington Old Hall liegt wie eine Oase in der neuerbauten Stadt Washington, die zwischen Durham und Newcastle liegt. Washington Hall ist der Familiensitz von Georg Washington's Vorfahren und wurde im Jahre 1937 mit amerikanisch-englischen Geldern liebevoll restauriert.

Übersetzung Ingrid C. Whale

North Northumberland and the Coast

Northumberland

Heatherland and bent land
Black land and white
God bring me to Northumberland
The land of my delight

Land of singing waters
And words from off the sea
God bring me to Northumberland
The land where I would be

Heather land and bent land
And valleys rich with corn
God bring me to Northumberland
The land where I was born.

Wilfrid Wilson Gibson

Yeavering Bell

Just to see the rain
Sweeping over Yeavering Bell
Once again!

Just to see again
Light break over Yeavering Bell
After rain.

Wilfrid Wilson Gibson

From **Winter in Northumberland**

Through fell and moorland
And salt-sea foreland
Our noisy norland
Resounds and rings
Waste waves thereunder
Are blown in sunder,
And winds make thunder
With cloudwide wings.

Sea-drift makes dimmer
The beacon's glimmer;
Nor sail nor swimmer
Can try the tides;
And snowdrifts thicken
Where, when leaves quicken,
Under the heather the sundew hides.

Algernon Charles Swinburne

The Shining Strand

This is the kind of day Northumberland excels in:
High clouds, a golden wind and waves of dancing sun,
The weft of land and sea that ancient legend dwells in
Glancing with battles royal fought bravely lost or won.

The broken chapel sunk under the sheep-cropped grasses
Stirs to the bracing hymn of curlew on the air.
The saints' and hermits' bones quiver as once more passes
The rush of shining peace fragrant with praise and prayer.

This is the kind of peace that set St Aidan building,
That blessed the skirmishes of foray and of feud.
All courage and high heart, its surges still come yielding
The flying buttress hope, and pele tower fortitude.

J. Phoenice

From **Briggflatts**

Shepherds follow the links,
sweet turf studded with thrift;
fell-born men of precise instep
leading demure dogs
from Tweed and Till and Teviotdale,
with hair combed back from the muzzle,
dogs from Redesdale and Coquetdale
taught by Wilson and Telfer.
Their teeth are white as birch
slow under black fringe
of silent, accurate lips.
The ewes are heavy with lamb.
Snow lies bright on Hedgehope
and tacky mud about Till
where the fells have stepped aside
and the river praises itself,
silence by silence sits
and Then is diffused in Now.

Light lifts from the water.
Frost has put rowan down,
a russet blotch of bracken
tousled about the trunk.
Bleached sky. Cirrus
reflects sun that has left
nothing to badger eyes

Basil Bunting

From **In the Cheviots**

We walked on the backs of the sleeping mountains,
Coming to them through quiet valleys
By tracks fringed with flowers;
We followed shallow streams where cattle stood
Knee-deep in cool water, or under trees,
Dense domes of leaf;
And stone houses rested
As if they had grown out of the earth
Each with a quilt of fields around it,
To where the hills had laid themselves down
In a circle, with their heads together.

Margaret Wilkes

*Basil Bunting (1900-85), poet and translator, was born and educated in Newcastle and is now acknowledged as one of the great English poets of his time. His masterpiece was **Briggflatts** (1966), a long autobiographical poem.*

*Wilfrid Wilson Gibson (1878-1962), 'the people's poet', belonged to a well-known Hexham family and many of his poems deal with the life of people of the north of England and its landscape. He gained a national reputation with the publication of his **Collected Poems** (1926)*

*J. Phoenice lived in North Northumberland and her poetry was published by the Oriel Press. 'The Shining Strand' appeared in **From the Kyloe Hills** (1970).*

*Algernon Charles Swinburne (1837-1909), poet, was the grandson of Sir John Edward Swinburne, 6th baronet, of Capheaton and spent many of his school holidays in Northumberland. He became a close friend of Lady Pauline Trevelyan of Wallington and a member of her circle of writers and artists. Most of the poems here are taken from his **Ballads of the English Border** ed. W. A. Maclehose (1925)*

Margaret Wilkes lives in Northumberland where she paints and writes.

Berwick-upon-Tweed *I*
From the south, showing the
17th-century Old Bridge.

2 **Berwick-upon-Tweed**
Old Bridge, with swans
and fishing boat.

Berwick-upon-Tweed *3*
Royal Border bridge
showing (on the left)
remains of the
medieval castle.

4 **Ford Church**
13th-century church, in the castle
grounds, with the gateway to the
castle in the background.

Norham Castle 5
The keep from the gatehouse,
showing medieval walls. Norham
was the chief northern stronghold
of the Bishops of Durham.

6 **The Cheviot**
With Comb Fell
and Hedgehope Hill
from Cold Law.

Chillingham Castle 7

From the south, showing the
former chapel on the right. The
castle dates from the 14th century.
In the park is the last herd of
English wild cattle.

8

Lindisfarne Priory
West entrance to the ruins of the
priory, built in the first half of the
12th century when monks
returned to the site of St Aidan's
monastery, after the Danish
invasions.

Lindisfarne Castle, Holy Island *9*
From the shore. A small 16th-
century fort with original outside
walls, on a dramatic outcrop of the
Whin Sill. Converted in 1902 by
the architect Edwin Lutyens.

10 **Bamburgh Castle**
From the sand dunes, in autumn.
'For rugged strength and barbaric
grandeur, it is the king of
Northumbrian castles'. The castle
was bought by Lord Crewe,
Bishop of Durham, in 1704 and
was restored by his trustees.

Bamburgh Beach
Looking out from the dunes
to the Farne Islands.

II

12 **Seahouses Harbour**
Showing the village and early
19th-century limekilns, now used
as fishermen's stores.

Beadnell Harbour *13*
At sunset.

14 **The Cheviots and Wooler**
From Weetwood Bank,
showing the river Till.

Dunstanburgh Castle from Embleton Bay

15

The castle was started in 1314 after the English lost Berwick to the Scots at Bannockburn.

16 Roughting Linn
Cup-and-ring carvings from the
late Neolithic or early Bronze Age
(end of third millennium BC). The
largest of these carved rocks in
northern England, easily accessible
from the Wooler to Berwick road.

The Aln, Coquet and the Wansbeck

Stones trip Coquet burn:
grass trails, tickles
till her glass thrills

The breeze she wears
lifts and falls back
Where beasts cool

in midgy shimmer
she dares me chase
under a bridge,

giggles, ceramic
huddle of notes,
darts from gorse

and I follow, fooled.
She must rest, surely;
some steep pool

to plodge or dip
and silent taste
with all my skin.

Basil Bunting

The crowning county of England – yes, the best! . .
Have you and I, then, raced across its moors
Till horse and boy were well-nigh mad with glee
So often, summer and winter, home from school,
And not found that out? Take the streams away
The country would be sweeter than the south
Anywhere: give the south our streams, would it
Be fit to match our borders? Flower and crag,
Burnside and boulder, heather and whin – you don't
Dream you can match them south of this?

Algernon Charles Swinburne

Nae more we'll fish the coaly Tyne
Nae mair the oozy Team
Nae mair we'll try the sedgy Pont,
Or Derwent's woody stream;
But we'll awa' to Coquet-side,
For Coquet bangs them a',
Whose winding streams sae sweetly glide
By Brinkburn's bonny ha'.

Thomas Doubleday

From **Alnwick**

South of the strawberry moors where the lions have
straight tails,
I came on an old pant and being thirsty
Wedged my head between the beasts' and drew up paps
of water
With wild mouth sucking.

Under the arch of horn I drank
Deeper than a bridgroom of bliss in the heat,
And felt on my face and shoulders garlands
Of rough brown arum lilies.

J. C. Grant

From **A Jacobite's Exile (1746)**

On Aikenshaw the sun blinks braw
The burn rins blithe and fain
There's nought wi' me I wadna gie
To look thereon again.

On Keilder-side the wind blaws wide:
There sounds nae hunting-horn
That rings sae sweet as the winds that beat
Round banks where Tyne is born.

The Wansbeck sings with all her springs,
The banks and braes give ear
And the wood that rungs wi' the sang she sings
I may no see nor hear
For far and far thae blithe burns are
And strange is a'thing near.

The light there lightens, the day there brightens,
The loud wind there lives free
Nae light comes nigh me or wind blaws by me
That I wae hear or see.

Algernon Charles Swinburne

*Thomas Doubleday (1790-1870), poet, radical politician and
merchant, was born and died in Newcastle. As a poet, he is best
known for his angling songs, notably the **Fisher's Garlands**, written
with Robert Roxby. These lines are part of a broadside published in
1821.*

*J. C. Grant was born in Alnwick, Northumberland, in 1898. He was a
civil servant and the author of a controversial novel about a pit village
(**The Back-to-Backs**, 1930). 'Alnwick' and 'The Tides of Tyne'
appeared in his collection, **Plough and Coble** (1967).*

Alnwick Castle *17*
From the river Aln. Seat of the
Dukes of Northumberland.
The castle has belonged to the
Percy family since the
14th century and was much
restored in the
18th and 19th centuries.

18 Hulne Priory in Hulne Park

One of the earliest Carmelite
foundations, built in 1242 by
William de Vesci. The 15th-century
curtain wall and square gatehouse
can be seen.

Alnwick Castle *19*
From the Lion Bridge,
looking across the park
landscaped by Lancelot
(Capability) Brown, *c.* 1765.

20 **Edlingham Castle**
The remains of a small fortified
manor, with moated enclosure of
the 14th century, showing the
tower and lower walls.

**Cup-and-ring carved rock
at Lordenshaws
on Garleigh Moor** *21*

The finest of these carvings with
the Simonside Hills in the distance.

22 **Warkworth Castle**

Probably built originally by Henry, son of King David of Scotland, who was made Earl of Nothumberland in 1139. The castle has belonged to the Percy family since 1332 and most of the present building dates from after the Scottish invasion of 1383.

Amble Harbour *23*
With boats.

24 **The Coquet river**
Near Shillmoor. The area is owned
by the Ministry of Defence, and is
easily explored from car parks and
footpaths by agreement between
Northumberland National Park
and the Ministry.

Cragside

From the garden, with rhododendrons. Dramatic country house designed by the architect Norman Shaw for the first Lord Armstrong and built 1870-85. Lord Armstrong was the greatest arms manufacturer of his time and an inventor especially interested in water power.

26 **Brinkburn Priory**
The Augustinian priory (right) was
founded between 1130 and 1135
and restored in 1858-9. On the left
is the manor house, originally part
of the monastic buildings and
remodelled in the Gothic style
in 1810.

View north to Cheviots *27*
From the summit of Simonside
Hill. The Simonside and Cheviot
Hills lie within Northumberland
National Park.

28 **Harbottle Castle**
Remains of the castle, built around
1157 by the Umfraville family to
control the routes through upper
Coquetdale. One of the finest
medieval earthworks in the county.
The Harbottle Hills are
in the distance.

Lady's Well, Holystone

The name comes from the nunnery founded by the Benedictines in 1124. The well is associated with the border saint, Ninian, and may have been a watering place on the road to the coast. The statue represents St Paulinus who, according to legend, conducted a mass baptism here.

30 **Morpeth Court House**
From Carlisle Park. Built 1822-8,
as the gateway to the
former county gaol.

Bothal Castle *31*
On a spur overlooking the
Wansbeck, probably dating from
the mid 14th century and restored
in the 19th century.

32 **Mitford Castle**
In the snow. Remains of the
12th-century castle, on a hill above
the Wansbeck.

Newminster Abbey
33
A re-erected arch, part of the
remains of an important
12th-century Cistercian Abbey
near Morpeth, now a
romantic ruin.

34 **Belsay Quarry Garden**
Showing leaves of *Gunnera
mantica*. This magical garden
was created by Sir Charles Monck
in the quarry which provided
the stone for Belsay Hall,
built between 1807 and 1817.

35

Belsay Castle with Manor House

From the south-west. Belsay, with
its castle, Grecian mansion,
gardens and lake, all created by the
Middleton family, is one of the
most interesting properties in the
country. It is now in the care of
English Heritage.

36 **Wallington Hall in snow**
Built by the merchant and banker,
Sir William Blackett, in 1688 and
altered in the 18th and 19th
centuries. The dragon heads are
said to have been brought from
London as ballast in one of the
Blacketts' coal barges.

Bolam Lake *37*
In the grounds of Bolam Hall and
now part of a country park.

38 **Elsdon**

'The capital of Redesdale when neither Scotland nor England existed'. The 'vicar's pele' in the background was probably built in the early 15th century by the Umfraville family.

The Tyne and Hadrian's Wall

From **The Tides of Tyne**

Tender as the tides of Tyne
In the salmon-time of spring when the river
Was a flowing rock with grains of silver
Dark Hadrian came.
        It was his heart
That was homesick-tender as he turned to look back
At his ships lying beached on the bank, their seams
Still white lines of salt he fondly dreamt
They had brought from his warm, blue, Roman seas;
Not yet a nightmare with the salt seams turned
To bonds of snow by the savage frost,
Binding boat and man to this wintry land.

....

        Did they dream
Of the great wall finished and peaceful years
In closest friendship with the native folk,
And local lasses loved and bearing
Their children, founding a race, half Roman
And half Northumbrian, the blood
Still blended in our veins today, still changing
The lonely shepherd leaning on his crook
Into a Roman leaning on his spear
In the eerie dusk? Or you might see
Another of these Geordies in the busy town,
His northern dourness suddenly dispersed
Before the onrush of his Latin blood,
As merry on a dark wet Saturday night
(Relic of Saturnalian sprees),
He dances with the lads down Grainger Street
Home to Wallsend with its clanging ships
Buckling their breastplates to great ribs of steel,
As once the Romans put on their clanging armour
To build fresh fame beside the coal-dark Tyne.

J. C. Grant

Hareshaw

The heather's black on Hareshaw
When Redesdale's lying white
When grass is green in Redesdale
Dark Hareshaw blossoms bright.

They harvest hay in Redesdale
For beasts within the byre
The heather upon Hareshaw
Is harvested with fire.

Wilfrid Wilson Gibson

From **On the Great Wall**

The houses change from gardened villas to shut forts
with watch-towers of grey stone, and great stone-walled
sheepfolds, guarded by armed Britons of the North
Shore. In the naked hills beyond the naked houses, where
the shadows of the clouds play like cavalry charging, you
see puffs of black smoke from the mines. The hard road
goes on and on – past altars to Legions and Generals
forgotten, and broken statues of Gods and Heroes, and
thousands of graves where the mountain foxes and hares
peep at you. Red-hot in summer, freezing in winter, is
that big purple heather country of broken stone.

Rudyard Kipling

From **A Jacobite's Farewell (1716)**

There's nae mair lands to tyne, my dear,
And nae mair lives to gie
Though a man think sair to live mae mair,
There's but one day to die.

For a' things come and a' days gane
What needs ye rend your hair?
But kiss me till the morn's morrow,
Then I'll kiss ye nae mair.

O lads are lost and life' losing,
And what were they to gie?
Fu' mony a man gives all he can,
But nae man else gives ye.

Our king wons ower the sea's water,
And I in prison sair:
But I'll win out the morn's morrow,
And ye'll see me nae mair.

Algernon Charles Swinburne

Derwentwater's Farewell

Farewell to pleasant Dilston Hall,
My father's ancient seat;
A stranger now must call thee his,
Which gars my heart to greet.

No more along the banks of Tyne
I'll rove in autumn gray
No more I'll hear at early dawn
The laverock wake the day
Farewell, farewell, George Collingwood,
Since fate has put us down,
If thou and I have lost our lives
King James has lost his crown

Albeit that here in London town
It is fate to die;
O carry me to Northumberland
In my father's grave to lie
There chant my solemn requiem
In Hexham's holy towers
And let six maids of fair Tynedale
Scatter my grave with flowers.

Robert Surtees

From **A Memoir of Thomas Bewick written by Himself**

As soon as I filled all the blank places in my books, I had recourse at all spare times to the gravestones and the floor of the church porch with a bit of chalk to give vent to this propensity of mine of figuring whatever I had seen. At that time I had never heard of the word 'drawing' nor did I know of any other paintings besides the King's Arms in the church, and the signs in Ovingham of the Black Bull, the White Horse, the Salmon and the Hounds and Hare. I always thought I could make a far better hunting scene than the latter; the others were beyond my hand . . . But my propensity for drawing was so rooted that nothing could deter me from persevering in it; and many of my evenings at home were spent in filling the flags of the floor and the hearthstone with my chalky designs.

Thomas Bewick, wood engraver, was born at Cherryburn, near Prudhoe, in 1753. He is buried in Ovingham churchyard. He is famous for his detailed engravings of birds, animals and local life.

*Rudyard Kipling (1865-1936), journalist, novelist and poet. The description of the Wall, put into the mouth of a Roman soldier, is taken from a story in **Puck of Pook's Hill** (1906)*

Robert Surtees (1774-1834) of Mainsforth, Co. Durham, was a celebrated antiquary and topographer who also composed ballads, some of which he persuaded his friend, Sir Walter Scott, to accept as authentic.

39

Hadrian's Wall
West of Housesteads, in snow
and mist.

40 **Hadrian's Wall**
At Winshield Crags, in frost.

Hadrian's Wall
At Walltown Crags. *41*

42 **Black Middens Bastle House**
Tarset Burn.

Kielder Water *43*
From Otterstone viewpoint, Bull
Crag Peninsula.

44 Blanchland Abbey

Founded for the
Premonstratensian Canons in 1165.
The charming village, created out
of the monastic buildings in the
18th century, is said to have been
named after the white robes of the
monks.

Hexham Abbey
45
From the park. The first church
was founded by Wilfrid in the
7th century and was rebuilt
as a priory church after 1113. It
was restored in the 19th century.

46 **Chesters**
The Bath House at the Roman
fort of Cilurnum which was
built to guard the bridge
over the river Tyne.

Chollerford *47*
River Tyne, in snow and hoar frost, at the place where the Military Road crosses the river. The Roman bridge at Chesters can be reached by a footpath along the river bank.

48 **Corbridge**
From the river, showing the
17th-century stone bridge,
the only Tyne bridge to survive
the flood of 1771.

Corbridge *49*
The village seen from the Roman
garrison town. In the foreground
are granaries, bordering Stanegate.

50 **Aydon Castle**
Originally a 13th-century hall,
beautifully placed above the steep,
wooded banks of the Cor Burn.

Dilston
Ruins of the castle, incorporated
into a wing of Dilston Hall *c.* 1620
(now destroyed). The last home
of James, last Earl of
Derwentwater, executed for his
part in the 1715 rebellion.

52 **Matfen**
Prehistoric standing stone,
decorated with cup marks.

Chipchase Castle *53*
In lovely country, above the
North Tyne. A 14th-century
tower and a Jacobean house,
altered in the 18th century.

54 **Prudhoe Castle**
From the south, showing the keep, gatehouse and barbican. Built by the Umfraville family and dating from the late 12th century.

St Andrew's Church, Bywell *55*
The smaller of two churches dating
from the Saxon period. The village
has disappeared but Bywell
remains one of the most beautiful
places in the Tyne valley.

56 **Langley Castle**
Probably a 14th-century
remodelling of an earlier hall
house; destroyed by Henry IV in
1405 and impressively restored by
the distinguished local historian,
Cadwallader Bates, in the 1890s.

Allen Banks *57*
In the Ridley Woods, on the banks
of the river Allen.

58

Hareshaw Linn
A lovely waterfall, north of
Bellingham, where the Hareshaw
burn joins the North Tyne. It is
owned by Northumberland
National Park and can be reached
by a delightful woodland path
along the burn.

Tyneside, Teesdale and the Wear

The Keel Row

As I went up Sandgate, up Sandgate, up Sandgate,
As I went up Sandgate I heard a lassie sing –
Weel may the keel row, the keel row, the keel row,
Weel may the keel row that my laddies's in!

He wears a blue bonnet, blue bonnet, blue bonnet,
He wears a blue bonnet, a dimple in his chin:
And weel may the keel row, the keel row,
And weel may the keel row that my laddies's in!

Newcastle's paramount claim to attention is that in the whole world there is not a more stirring monument to human energy than is presented by the town and its river, the Tyne . . . the fitting eulogy of Newcastle would be a recital of the names of the great shipbuilding and other works on the Tyne, the array of inventions and discoveries which trod hot on the heels of Stephenson's first locomotive, and the bulk of goods manufactured by those armies of labour which man the innumerable works.

Peter Anderson Graham, 1920.

Blaydon Races

Aw went to Blaydon Races, 'twas on the ninth of Joon,
Eighteen hundred an' sixty-two, on a summer's efternoon;
Aw tyuk the 'bus frae Balmbra's, an' she wis heavy laden,
Away we went alang Collingwood Street, that's on the road to Blaydon.

O lads, ye shud only seen us gannin',
We pass'd the foaks upon the road just as they wor stannin';
Thor wes lots o' lads an' lasses there, all wi' smiling faces
Gawn alang the Scotswood Road, to see the Blaydon Races.

*The 'Keel Row' has been described as the Tyneside National Anthem. George Ridley's 'Blaydon Races', of which only the first verse and chorus is printed here, is equally well known. The text is taken from Allan's **Illustrated Edition of Tyneside Songs and Readings** (1891)*

Durham

Durham is one of the great experiences of Europe to those who appreciate architecture . . . The group of Cathedral, Castle and Monastery on the rock can only be compared to Avignon and Prague.

Nikolaus Pevsner, 1953

The view from the castle itself at the top of a steep hill is very grand and Edinburghesque; but when you cross the Wear by the Prebends' Bridge and, ascending through its beautiful skirt of wood, plant yourself on the hill opposite the cathedral, the view of the cathedral and castle together is superb; even Oxford has no view to compare with it. The country, too, has a strong turbulent roll in it, which smacks of the north and of neighbouring mountains, which greatly delighted me . . . I was most agreeably disappointed for I had fancied Durham rising out of a cinder bed.

Matthew Arnold, Letter to his Mother, 1860

As the train swung round a curve and over a viaduct, my breath was completely taken away for an instant by the sight of Durham cathedral . . . It seemed to float proudly above the smoky rooftops, gradually turning on its own axis as we described an arc around it, in order, so it seemed, to show itself off to the best advantage. The massive towers, the age-mellowed stone whose colour blended so naturally with that of the foliage around it on the banks of the river Wear; above all, the mute drama of human faith and achievement played on a stage set by God in the elbow of a river and watched over by the vigilance of eight centuries; all this gave me a starting-point for my new studies and so helped me to forget my temporary sense of loneliness.

William Conton, 1960

Matthew Arnold (1822-88), poet, critic and educator, is now best known for his poetry.

*William Conton, was an African student at Durham University who wrote about his experiences in England in **The African** (1960).*

*Sir Nikolaus Pevsner, was an architectural historian and author of **The Buildings of England** (46 volumes, 1951-74). Many of these books have since been expanded and revised and are essential reading for any student of English buildings.*

59

Durham Cathedral
Through trees from South Street.

60
Durham Castle gatehouse

Durham Cathedral and Old Fulling Mill *61*

From the river Wear.

62   **Bishop Auckland Palace**
A romantic view of the Bishop's
Palace seen through the screen
wall and inner gateway of 1796.
The Palace was badly damaged in
the Civil War of the 17th century,
and much restored in the 1750s.

**Bishop Auckland Palace.
The Deer House** *63*

Built in 1767, north of the palace.
A walled enclosure for deer
who sheltered between the inner
wall and arcaded outer wal!.

64 **Escomb Church**
One of only three complete
Saxon churches surviving
in Britain.

Finchale Priory

Through autumn leaves, showing the prior's lodgings (on the left) and the chapter house (on the right). Built in a loop of the river Wear, surrounded by trees, the abbey was used as a holiday hostel for Durham monks in the 14th century.

66 Killhope Wheel Lead Mining Centre

Showing the 40ft (12m.) diameter cast-iron water wheel.

Weardale *67*
Showing Cowshill
and Killhope Burn.

68 **Barnard Castle**
From the Inner Ward, showing
(from the left) Mortham's 5-storey
tower, hall and Round Tower.
A major castle, dating from
1125-40. Dismantled by the
Vane family, who acquired it
in the 1620s to repair Raby.

Bowes Museum *69*
Designed in the French
Renaissance style for John Bowes
(1811-85), son of the 10th Earl of
Strathmore, to house his collection
of paintings and furniture. Started
in 1865 and opened in 1892.

70 **Egglestone Abbey**

From the river Tees, showing
the east end of the church and
16th-century house, rebuilt from
the monastic buildings. On the
right, the two storey lavatories
building.

High Force *71*
Spectacular waterfall on the moors
of Upper Teesdale in a National
Nature Reserve.

72 **Washington Old Hall**
The family home of George
Washington, rebuilt in 1613 from
the ruins of an earlier house.
Restored in 1937 and furnished in
17th-century style.

Raby Castle

Fortified seat of the Neville family, whose chief military stronghold was at Brancepeth. The first Lord Barnard (whose family, the Vanes, have owned the estate since 1616) tried to demolish the castle in 1714 to spite his heir but was forced to rebuild it.

74 **Seaton Delaval Hall**
The last masterpiece (1718-29) of
Sir John Vanburgh, architect and
playwright. The house was twice
damaged by fire.

Marsden Rock *75*
On the Tyne and Wear coast,
about 2 miles (3.2km) from
the mouth of the Tyne.

76 **Tynemouth Priory**
From the entrance. Built on a steep cliff above the sea and acting as a fortress as well as a monastery throughout the Middle Ages.

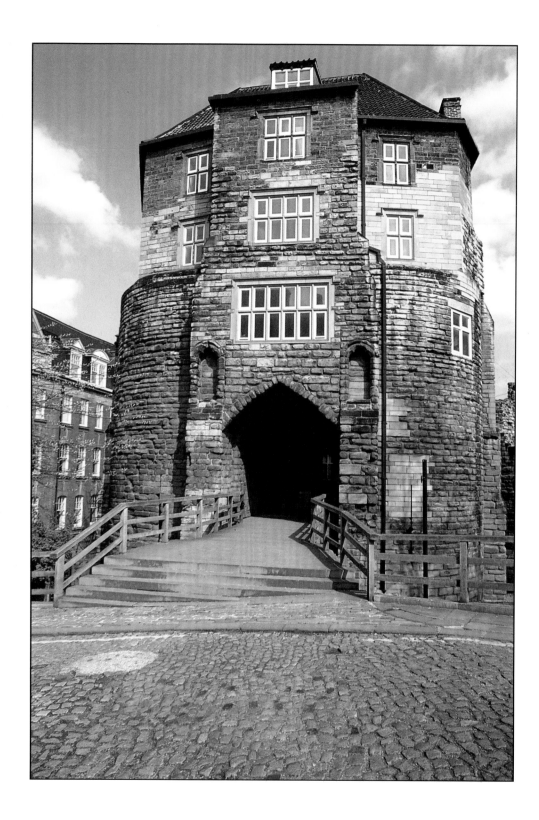

77

**The Black Gate,
Newcastle upon Tyne**

Gate to the castle, dating from
1247 and now housing the library
of the Society of Antiquaries
of Newcastle.

78

**The Civic Centre,
Newcastle upon Tyne**
Showing the banqueting hall and
(left) the Council chamber with the
sculpture of the Tyne river god
by David Wynne.

80

Tall Ships
at the Quayside
Newcastle upon Tyne